# Created AND REDEEMED

## THE UNIVERSAL MESSAGE OF JOHN PAUL II'S THEOLOGY OF THE BODY

*An Adult Faith Formation Program*

**Study Guide**

by Christopher West

Christopher West is a visiting lecturer at St. John Vianney Seminary in Denver, an adjunct professor of the Institute of Priestly Formation in Omaha, and a visiting professor of the John Paul II Institute for Studies on Marriage and Family in Melbourne Australia. His books (*Good News About Sex & Marriage* and *Theology of the Body Explained*), extensive lecturing, and numerous tapes have sparked an international groundswell of interest in John Paul II's theology of the body. He and his wife, Wendy, have three children.

© 2004 by Christopher West
All rights reserved. This study-guide may not be reproduced without permission.

All Scripture quotations are taken from the Revised Standard Version of the Bible, copyright 1946, 1952, 1971 by the Division of Christian Education of the National Council of Churches of Christ in the USA.

## Other Resources by Christopher West

Books:
 *Good News About Sex & Marriage: Answers to Your Honest Questions about Catholic Teaching* (Servant, 2000)
 *Crash Course in the Theology of the Body: A Study Guide* (Luminous Media, 2003)
 *Theology of the Body Explained: A Commentary on John Paul II's 'Gospel of the Body'*
  (Pauline Books & Media, 2003)
 *Theology of the Body for Beginners: A Basic Introduction to Pope John Paul II's Theological Timebomb*
  (Ascension Press, 2004)

Audio & Video Productions:
 Luminous Media is Christopher West's official distributor of audio and video presentations. Visit ChristopherWest.com or LuminousMedia.org for more information or call 800-376-0520.

For speaking engagements visit ChristopherWest.com and click on "speaking."

# Contents

*Talk 1:*
    Theology of the Body: An Education in Being Human ......................................... 1

*Talk 2:*
    *Created* as Male & Female: God's Original Plan ...................................................... 7

*Talk 3:*
    *Redeemed* as Male & Female: Christ Restores God's Plan ..................................... 12

*Talk 4:*
    The Heavenly Marriage & the Joy of Christian Celibacy ........................................ 16

*Talk 5:*
    The Two Become "One Flesh": Living the "Great Mystery" of Marriage ........ 20

*Talk 6:*
    Authentic Chastity: From Legalism to Liberty ........................................................ 24

*Talk 7:*
    Theology in the Bedroom: Love, Sex, & Fertility ..................................................... 28

*Talk 8:*
    "Put out into the Deep": The New Evangelization ................................................. 32

# Abbreviations

**CCC**     *Catechism of the Catholic Church*, Second Edition (Libreria Editrice Vaticana, 1997)

**CTH**     *Crossing the Threshold of Hope*, John Paul II (Knopf, 1994)

**EM**     *Ecclesia in America*, John Paul II's Apostolic Exhortation on the Church in America (Pauline, 1999)

**EV**     *Evangelium Vitae*, John Paul II's Encyclical Letter on the Gospel of Life (Pauline, 1995)

**FC**     *Familiaris Consortio*, John Paul II's Apostolic Exhortation on the Christian Family (Pauline, 1981)

**FR**     *Fides et Ratio*, John Paul II's Encyclical Letter on Faith and Reason (Pauline, 1998)

**GS**     *Gaudium et Spes*, Vatican II's Pastoral Constitution on the Church in the Modern World (Pauline, 1965)

**KW**     *Karol Wojtyla: The Thought of the Man Who Became John Paul II*, Rocco Buttiglione (Eerdman's, 1997)

**LF**     *Letter to Families*, John Paul II's Letter in the Year of the Family (Pauline, 1994)

**LR**     *Love & Responsibility*, Karol Wojtyla's (John Paul II's) philosophical work on sexuality (Ignatius Press, 1993)

**MD**     *Mulieris Dignitatem*, John Paul II's Apostolic Letter on the Dignity and Vocation of Women (Pauline, 1988)

**NMI**     *Novo Millennio Ineunte*, John Paul II's Apostolic Letter at the Close of the Jubilee Year (Pauline, 2001)

**RM**     *Redemptoris Missio*, John Paul II's Encyclical Letter on the Mission of the Redeemer (Pauline, 1990)

**SE**     *Springtime of Evangelization:* John Paul II's 1998 ad Limina Addresses to the Bishops of the United States (Ignatius, 1998)

**SL**     *The Splendor of Love: John Paul II's Vision for Marriage & Family*, Walter J. Schu (New Hope, 2003)

**TB**     *The Theology of the Body*, John Paul II's addresses on Human Love in the Divine Plan (Pauline 1997)[1]

**VS**     *Veritatis Splendor*, John Paul II's encyclical letter on the Splendor of Truth (Pauline, 1993)

**WH**     *Witness to Hope*, George Weigel's biography of Pope John Paul II (Harper Collins, 1999)

---

[1] For ease of reference, page numbers provided refer to this edition. However, please note that the 1997 one-volume edition of the Pope's catechesis was copyedited and may differ slightly from the original Vatican translation quoted in this study guide.

*Talk 1*

# Theology of the Body:

*An Education in Being Human*

## 1. The Foundation of Human Life

In every age men and women – even if sometimes only secretly – have been fascinated with sex.

> **1a.** "Why in the world are we so consumed by [sex]? The impulse to procreate may lie at the heart of [it], but ...bursting from our sexual center is a whole spangle of other things – art, song, romance, obsession, rapture, sorrow, companionship, love, even violence and criminality – all playing an enormous role in everything from our physical [and] emotional health to our politics, our communities, our very life spans. Why should this be so? Did nature simply overload us in the mating department...? Or is there something smarter and subtler at work, some larger interplay among sexuality, life and what it means to be human?" (*Time* Magazine, Jan 19, 2004, p. 64).

The issue of sex is no footnote in human life. It is a question of utmost importance to each and every one of us, and to the survival of civilization itself.

> **1b.** The call to communion inscribed in our sexuality is "the fundamental element of human existence in the world" (TB, 16), "the foundation of human life" (EM, n. 46), and, hence, "the deepest substratum [foundation] of human ethics and culture"(TB, 163).

Sexual attitudes and behaviors have the power to orient not only individuals, but entire nations and societies toward respect for life – or toward its utter disregard.

> **1c.** "It is an illusion to think we can build a true culture of human life if we do not ...accept and experience sexuality and love and the whole of life according to their true meaning and their close interconnection" (EV, n. 97).

In short, as sex goes, so go marriage and the family. As marriage and the family go, so goes the world. Such logic does not bode well for today's culture.

- If the task of the 20th century was to rid itself of the Christian sexual ethic, the task of the 21st century must be to reclaim it.

- But the often repressive approach of previous generations of Christians isn't going to suffice.

- We need a fresh approach that reveals the *beauty* of God's plan for sex and the *joy* of living it.

NOTES

- God grants the Church what she needs when she needs it.

The "theology of the body" is a collection of 129 short talks John Paul II delivered early in his pontificate on the meaning of the human body, sex, and marital love.

- Yet, it is not only for the married. Nor is it only for Catholics.
- The message of the theology of the body is *universal*.
- It reveals precisely that "larger interplay among sexuality, life, and what it means to be human."

**1d.** Though it focuses on sexual love, the theology of the body affords "the rediscovery of the meaning of the whole of existence, the meaning of life" (TB, 168).

**1e.** The theology of the body is "one of the boldest reconfigurations of Catholic theology in centuries" – "a kind of *theological time bomb* set to go off with dramatic consequences ...perhaps in the twenty-first century" (WH, 336, 343).

## 2. Understanding the Body as a "Theology"

We cannot see God. As pure Spirit, God is totally beyond our vision. Yet Christians believe that the invisible God has made himself visible. How?

**2a.** In "the body of Jesus 'we see our God made visible and so are caught up in love of the God we cannot see'" (CCC, n. 477).

God's mystery revealed in human flesh – the theology *of the body*: this is not only a series of talks by John Paul II. This is the very "logic" of Christianity.

**2b.** "Through the fact that the Word of God became flesh the body entered theology ...through the main door" (TB, 89).

**2c.** "The body, in fact, and it alone, is capable of making visible what is invisible: the spiritual and divine. It was created to transfer into the visible reality of the world, the mystery hidden since time immemorial in God, and thus to be a sign of it" (TB, 76).

## 3. God's Mystery & the Spousal Analogy

What is the mystery hidden in God that the body signifies? In a word – *communion*.

**3a.** "God has revealed his innermost secret: God himself is an eternal exchange of love, Father, Son, and Holy Spirit, and he has destined us to share in that exchange" (CCC, n. 221).

Scripture uses many images to describe God's love. Each has its own valuable place. But the spousal image is used far more than any other.

- The Bible begins and ends with marriages – Adam-Eve and Christ-Church.

- Spousal theology looks to the nuptial "book ends" of Genesis and Revelation as a key for interpreting what lies between.

- Through the lens of the spousal analogy we learn that God's eternal plan is to "marry" us (see Hos 2:19).

- God wanted this eternal plan of love and communion to be so obvious to us that he stamped an image of it in our very being by creating us as male and female.

"'For this reason a man shall leave his father and mother and be joined to his wife, and the two shall become one flesh.' This is a great mystery, and I mean in reference to Christ and the church" (Eph 5:21-32).

> **3b.** Understanding the true meaning of the body and sexuality "concerns the entire Bible" (TB, 249). It plunges us into "the perspective of the whole Gospel, of the whole teaching, in fact, of the whole mission of Christ" (TB, 175).

> **3c.** "John Paul's portrait of sexual love as an icon of the interior life of God has barely begun to shape the Church's theology, preaching, and religious education. When it does, it will compel a dramatic development of thinking about virtually every major theme in the Creed" (WH, 853)

Like all analogies, the image of sexual love, while very helpful, is also limited and inadequate.

> **3d.** "In no way is God in man's image. He is neither man nor woman. God is pure spirit in which there is no place for the difference between the sexes" (CCC, n. 370; see also nn. 42, 239).

> **3e.** God's mystery "remains transcendent in regard to [the spousal] analogy as in regard to any other analogy, whereby we seek to express it in human language" (TB, 330). At the same time, however, there "is no other human reality which corresponds more, humanly speaking, to that divine mystery" (homily, 12/30/88).

## 4. Battle for the Body

Satan seeks to counter God's plan by plagiarizing the sacraments (Tertullian).

- God's eternal plan for the body is union, communion, marriage; this brings life.
- Satan's counter-plan for the body is separation, fracture, divorce; this brings death.
- St. Paul's first words of advice: "gird your loins with the truth" (Eph 6:14).

**4a.** Marriage and the family are "placed at the center of the great struggle between good and evil, between life and death, between love and all that is opposed to love" (LF, n. 23).

## 5. Structure of the Teaching

Through an in-depth reflection on the Scriptures, John Paul seeks to answer two universal questions:

(1) "What does it mean to be human?"

(2) "How am I supposed to live my life in a way the brings true happiness?"

These questions frame the two main parts of the Pope's study. In turn, each of these two parts contains three "cycles" or subdivisions broken down as follows.

PART I: "What does it mean to be human?"

- Cycle 1: *Our Origin*. This concerns man's experience of the body and sex before sin. It's based on Christ's discussion with the Pharisees about God's plan for marriage "in the beginning" (see Mt 19:3-9).

- Cycle 2: *Our History*. This concerns man's experience of the body and sex affected by sin yet redeemed in Christ. It's based on Jesus' words in the Sermon on the Mount regarding adultery committed "in the heart" (see Mt 5:27-28).

- Cycle 3: *Our Destiny*. This concerns man's experience of the body and sex in the resurrection. It's based on Christ's discussion with the Sadducees regarding the body's resurrected state (see Mt 22:23-33).

PART II: "How am I supposed to live my life?"

- Cycle 4: *Celibacy for the Kingdom*. This is a reflection on Christ's words about those who renounce marriage for the kingdom of heaven (see Mt 19:12).

- Cycle 5: *Christian Marriage*. This is primarily a reflection on St. Paul's grand "spousal analogy" in Ephesians 5.

- Cycle 6: *Sexual Morality & Procreation*. In light of his preceding analysis, John Paul shifts the discussion on sexual morality from *legalism* ("How far can I go before I break the law?") to *liberty* ("What's the truth of sexuality that sets me *free* to love?").

**6. A Message of "Sexual Salvation"**

Those who have been turned-off by judgmental moralizers will find John Paul II's approach delightfully refreshing.

- The Pope imposes nothing and wags a finger at *no one*.
- He simply invites us to reflect with him on God's Word and our own experience to see if the love held out in the Scriptures is the love we really yearn for.
- It doesn't matter where we've been or what mistakes we've made. This is a message of "sexual salvation" – not condemnation.

୶

# Study Questions–Talk #1
# Theology of the Body:
# An Education in Being Human

1. Have you ever considered that we could understand *the body* as a "theology" (a study of God)?

2. Why is this teaching for all people and not just for married couples?

3. What is the effect of a culture's understanding of sexuality on its overall health?

4. In what ways does the body make visible things that are invisible?

5. In what ways might the human family "image" the Trinity: Father, Son, and Holy Spirit?

6. There are various images the Bible uses to describe God's love for us.

    - Why do you think the spousal image is used far more than any other?

NOTES

- How do you feel about the idea that God wants to "marry" us (see Hosea 2:19)?

7. What are some of the "counterfeits" we commonly accept in our culture? What would Jesus say to those pursuing counterfeit loves?

8. What are the two universal questions that Pope John Paul II seeks to answer through the Theology of the Body?

9. Why is it important to look at our origin, history, and destiny?

As you study the Theology of the Body, consider these age-old questions:

- Where do I come from and why do I exist?
- What is the meaning of life and how do I live it?
- What is my ultimate destiny and how do I attain it?
- Why is there evil in the world and how do I overcome it?

*Talk 2*

# Created As Male & Female:

## God's Original Plan

### CYCLE 1: OUR ORIGIN

**1. Christ Points us Back to "the Beginning"**

"For your hardness of heart Moses allowed you to divorce your wives, but from the beginning it was not so" (Mt 19:8).

- By starting with Christ's words, the Pope makes a specific statement.
- If our goal is to understand "who we are," we must turn to Christ.

**1a.** Christ "fully reveals man to himself and makes his supreme calling clear" (GS, n. 22).

**1b.** The "first man and the first woman must constitute ...the model ...for all men and women who, in any period, are united so intimately as to be 'one flesh'" (TB, 50).

**2. Man is "Alone" in the World (Original Solitude)**

"Then the Lord God said, 'It is not good that the man should be alone'" (Gen 2:18).

- This means not only that man is "alone" without the opposite sex, but that the human being (male and female) is "alone" in the visible world as a person.
- Adam realizes he's "different" from the animals. He's made in God's image. He has freedom – the capacity to choose between good and evil.
- Adam realizes his fundamental vocation: love of God and love of neighbor (see Lk 10:27).
- All this is experienced in the body.

**2a.** The "body expresses the person." It reveals "who man is (and who he should be)" (TB, 41).

**2b.** The man "might have reached the conclusion, on the basis of the experience of his own body, that he was substantially similar to the [animals]. But, on the contrary, ...he reached the conviction that he was 'alone'" (TB, 39).

### 3. Called to Live in Relationship (Original Unity)

Man "cannot fully find himself except through the sincere gift of himself" (GS, n. 24). "Therefore a man leaves his father and his mother and cleaves to his wife, and they become one flesh" (Gen 2:24).

- Their unity in "one flesh" is worlds apart from the copulation of animals. Unlike the animals, man and woman have the capacity to love (freedom).
- Therefore, like the experience of "solitude," unity also reveals that man and woman are created in God's image.

**3a.** Becoming "one flesh" refers not only to the joining of two bodies but is "a 'sacramental' expression which corresponds to the **communion of persons**" (TB, 123).

**3b.** "Man becomes the image of God not so much in the moment of solitude as in the moment of communion." In other words, man images God "not only through his own humanity, but also through the communion of persons which man and woman form right from the beginning.... On all this, right from the beginning, there descended the blessing of fertility linked with human procreation" (TB, 46).

### 4. Naked without Shame (Original Nakedness)

"And the man and his wife were both naked, and were not ashamed" (Gen 2:25).

- The Pope calls this the "key" for understanding God's original plan for man and woman (see TB, 52).
- They experienced sexual desire only as the desire to love in God's image. There's no shame (or fear) in love. "Perfect love casts out fear" (1 Jn 4:18).

**4a.** Nakedness reveals the **nuptial meaning of the body** which is the body's "capacity of expressing love: that love precisely in which the person becomes a gift and – by means of this gift – fulfills the very meaning of his being and existence" (TB, 63).

**4b.** "'Nakedness' signifies the original good of God's vision. It signifies ...the 'pure' value of humanity as male and female, the 'pure' value of the body and of sex" (TB, 57).

**4c.** Original nakedness demonstrates that "holiness entered the visible world." It is "in his body as male or female [that] man feels he is a subject of holiness." Holiness is what "enables man to express himself deeply with his own body... precisely by means of the 'sincere gift' of himself" (TB, 76-77).

## Cycle 2: Our History

### 5. Questioning the Gift (Original Sin)

"You will not die. For God knows that when you eat of it your eyes will be opened, and you will be like God, knowing good and evil" (Gn 3:4-5).

- When God is conceived of as a jealous tyrant, man is goaded to do battle against him so as not to be enslaved.
- Faith leads to "receptivity" before God. Lack of faith leads to "grasping."
- When we deny the gift in God, we lose our capacity to be a gift to one another.

**5a.** Woman "is the representative and the archetype of the whole human race: she *represents the humanity* which belongs to all human beings, both men and women" (MD, n. 4).

**5b.** The "paradigm of master-slave is foreign to the Gospel" (CTH, p. 226).

**5c.** By questioning love as God's motive in creation "man turns his back on ...'the Father.' In a way, he casts him out of his heart" (TB, 111).

**5d.** *"This is truly the key for interpreting reality. ...Original sin, then, attempts to abolish fatherhood"* (CTH, p. 228).

**5e.** If original sin is the denial of the gift, *"faith, in its deepest essence, is the openness of the human heart to the gift: to God's self-communication in the Holy Spirit"* (DV, n. 51).

### 6. The Entrance of Shame

When they disobeyed God "the eyes of both were opened, and they knew that they were naked; and they sewed fig leaves together and made themselves aprons. ...'I was afraid, because I was naked; and I hid myself" (Gen 3:7, 10).

- When God's love "died" in their hearts, sexual desire became inverted, self-seeking.
- Lust, therefore, is sexual desire void of God's love.
- Lust causes us almost to stoop back to the level of animals, yet we still know we're called to more – we're called to love.
- Lust, therefore, is a "reduction" of God's original plan. It doesn't offer more, but less.

NOTES

**6a.** "Man is ashamed of his body because of lust. In fact, he is ashamed not so much of his body as precisely of lust" (TB, 116).

**6b.** Shame also has a positive meaning as "a natural *form of self-defense for the person* against the danger of descending or being pushed into the position of an object for sexual use" (LR, 182).

**6c.** The 'heart' has become a battlefield between love and lust. The more lust dominates the heart, the less the [heart] experiences the nuptial meaning of the body" (TB, 126).

❧

# Study Questions–Talk #2
## *Created* As Male & Female: God's Original Plan

1. When speaking of divorce, Jesus tells us in Matthew 19:8 that "from the beginning it was not so." Does it seem possible that the suffering and sinfulness in the world is not how we were created to be?

2. Have you received a glimpse of how great your dignity is as a human person?

3. What does it mean to say, "Christ fully reveals man to himself"?

4. One of the key teachings of Vatican II states that "man cannot fully find himself except through the sincere gift of self." What does this mean?

5. In what primary way did Adam realize that he was "different" from the animals?

6. Becoming "one flesh" refers to much more than the joining of two bodies. Discuss the concept of "communion of persons."

6. John Paul II considers nakedness without shame as the key to understanding God's original plan for man and woman. To help you understand why, discuss the following questions:

   - Why were Adam and Eve not ashamed in their nakedness prior to the Fall?

   - What did their original nakedness signify?

- How did Adam and Eve experience sexual desire prior to the Fall?
- How did sexual desire change after the Fall?

7. Define 'lust.'

8. Why would we instinctively cover ourselves if a stranger were to enter into a room and see us unclothed?

9. Why is it difficult for us to see that our bodies are holy? Although the body is good and holy, why is it appropriate that we cover ourselves in a fallen world?

*Talk 3*

# Redeemed As Male & Female:

## Christ Restores God's Plan

**1. Adultery in the Heart**

"You have heard that it was said, 'You shall not commit adultery.' But I say to you that everyone who looks at a woman lustfully has already committed adultery with her in his heart" (Mt 5:27-28).

> **1a.** "Are we to fear the severity of these words, or rather have confidence in their salvific...power?" (TB, 159).
>
> **1b.** The heritage of our hearts "is deeper than the sinfulness inherited, deeper than lust....The words of Christ...reactivate that deeper heritage and give it real power in man's life" (TB, 168).
>
> **1c.** Christ calls us to experience "a real and deep victory" over the distortion of lust (see TB, 164). Christ wants to inspire our sexual desires "with everything that is noble and beautiful," with "the supreme value which is love" (see TB, 168).

**2. Freedom from the Law & the "New Ethos"**

If "you are led by the Spirit, you are not under the law" (Gal 5:18).

- We all know that laws, in and of themselves, do not change human hearts.
- Christ did not come to give us more "rules" to follow; he came to change our hearts (*ethos*) so that we would no longer need the rules.
- *Ethos* refers to our inner-world of values, what attracts and repulses us.
- In effect Christ says, "You've heard the commandment not to commit adultery, but the problem is you *desire* to commit adultery."
- Through ongoing conversion, the desires of our hearts gradually conform to God's law, to the point that we are "free from the law."

> **2a.** "The Law of the Gospel ...does not add new external precepts, but proceeds to reform the heart" (CCC, n. 1968). In "the Sermon on the

Mount ...the Spirit of the Lord gives new form to our desires" (CCC, n. 2764).

**2b.** "Christian ethos is characterized by a transformation of ...both man and woman, such as to express and realize the value of the body and sex according to the Creator's original plan" (TB, 163).

**2c.** The new ethos is "a living morality" in which we realize the very meaning of our humanity (see TB, 105).

**2d.** "The perfection of the moral good consists in man's being moved to the good not only by his will but also by his 'heart'" and even "by his sensitive appetite" (CCC, n. 1770, 1775).

## 3. The Redemption of the Body

We "groan inwardly as we wait for ...the redemption of our bodies" (Rom 8:23).

- St. Paul vividly describes the interior battle we all experience between good and evil (see Rom 7).
- But he also speaks of the power of redemption at work within us which is able to do far more than we ever think or imagine (see Eph 3:20).
- Balancing these truths, we find both a real battle with lust and the possibility of a real victory over it.

**2a.** The "'redemption of the body' is expressed not only in the resurrection as victory over death. It is present also in Christ's words addressed to 'historical' man... when ...Christ called man to overcome [lust] even in the ...movements of the human heart" (TB, 301).

**2b.** "Someone I was told, at the sight of a very beautiful body, felt impelled to glorify the Creator. The sight of it increased his love for God to the point of tears. Anyone who entertains such feelings in such circumstances is already risen ...before the general resurrection" (John Climacus, *The Ladder of Divine Assent*, 15th step, 58, p. 168).

**2c.** Christ's words about lust are "an invitation to a pure way of looking at others, capable of respecting the spousal [or nuptial] meaning of the body" (VS, n. 15).

## 4. Purity of Heart

"Blessed are the pure in heart, for they shall see God" (Mt 5: 8).

- Christian purity is not prudishness or puritanism!
- Mature Christian purity affords the ability to see God's mystery revealed in the human body and in man and woman's call to communion.

**3a.** "Purity is the glory of the human body before God. It is God's glory in the human body" (TB, 209).

**3b.** "Even now [purity of heart] enables us to see *according to* God...; it lets us perceive the human body – ours and our neighbor's – as a temple of the Holy Spirit, a manifestation of divine beauty" (CCC, n. 2519).

**3c.** Purity "is not just abstention." There is "another role of the virtue of purity ...more positive than negative." The positive dimension of purity "opens the way to a more and more perfect discovery of the dignity of the human body" (TB, 200; 213).

## 4. The Interpretation of Suspicion

Redemption does not magically remove the consequences of sin in this life. We still suffer, get ill, grow old, struggle with weaknesses and the pull of lust, etc. (see CCC, nn. 978, 1226, 1264, 1426). Yet, the reality of sin must not cause us to hold the human heart in continual suspicion.

- A "master of suspicion" is a person who does not know or does not fully believe in the transforming power of the Gospel.
- Lust holds sway in his own heart so he projects the same onto everyone else.
- In his mind the human body will always rouse lust; it can do nothing else.

**4a.** "Man cannot stop at putting the 'heart' in a state of continual and irreversible suspicion due to ...lust. ...Redemption is a truth, a reality, in the name of which man must feel called, and called with efficacy" (TB, 167).

**4b.** "The meaning of life is the antithesis of the interpretation 'of suspicion.' This interpretation is very different, it is radically different from what we discover in Christ's words in the Sermon on the Mount. These words reveal ...another vision of man's possibilities" (TB, 168).

*See next page for Study Questions*

# Study Questions–Talk #3
## *Redeemed* As Male & Female: Christ Restores God's Plan

1. The Pope chose to begin this section with the verse: "You have heard that is was said, 'You shall not commit adultery.' But I say to you that everyone who looks at a woman lustfully has already committed adultery with her in his heart" (Mt. 5:27-28). Why does the Pope say we should not fear the severity of Christ's words about lust?

2. Have you ever heard that Christ gives us "real power" to experience sexuality as the desire to love as God loves? Do you believe this?

3. What does "ethos" mean? Do you believe your ethos can actually change?

4. What is St. Paul referring to when he says we "groan inwardly as we wait... for the redemption of our bodies" (Rom. 8:23)?

5. Why do most people think of Christian morality as an oppressive list of rules? What does it mean to be "free from the law"?

6. In light of quotes 3a- 3c, what does it mean to say, "Blessed are the pure in heart, for they shall see God" (Mt. 5:8)?

7. Discuss the fine balance between taking too lightly that which may appear scandalous and the position taken by a "master of suspicion."

NOTES

NOTES

*Created & Redeemed – Page 16*

*Talk 4*

# The Heavenly Marriage & the Joy of Christian Celibacy

CYCLE 3: OUR DESTINY

### 1. Christ Points us to the Future

"For in the resurrection they neither marry nor are given in marriage" (Mt 22:30).

- Marriage exists only as a sign that's meant to point us to heaven, to the "Marriage of the Lamb" (Rev 19:7).
- In the resurrection, the sacrament will give way to the divine reality.
- This means the union of the sexes is not man's end-all-and-be-all. It's only an "icon."
- When we loose sight of our destiny, the *icon* inevitably becomes an *idol*.

**1a.** Marriage and procreation did not determine definitively the fundamental meaning of our creation as male and female. Marriage and procreation merely give a concrete expression to that meaning within history (see TB, 247).

### 2. The Beatific Vision

"For now we see in a mirror dimly, but then face to face" (1 Co 13:12).

- The beatific vision was foreshadowed (dimly, of course) right from the beginning in the union of man and woman.
- In the beatific vision, God will give himself totally to man, and we will respond with the total gift of ourselves to him.

**2a.** In "the resurrection we discover – in an [eternal] dimension – the same... nuptial meaning of the body ...in the meeting with the mystery of the living God ...face to face" (TB, 243).

**2b.** The beatific vision is "a concentration of knowledge and love on God himself." This knowledge "cannot be other than full participation in the interior life of God, that is, in the very trinitarian reality" (TB, 244).

**2c.** This "will be a completely new experience." Yet "at the same time it will not be alienated in any way from what man took part in from 'the beginning' nor from what, in the historical dimension [concerned] the procreative meaning of the body and sex" (TB, 248).

**2d.** "In the joys of their love [God gives spouses] here on earth a foretaste of the wedding feast of the Lamb" (CCC, n. 1642).

**2e.** The Church "longs to be united with Christ, her Bridegroom, in the glory of heaven" where she "will rejoice one day with [her] Beloved, in a happiness and rapture that can never end" (CCC, n. 1821).

## 3. The Communion of Saints

"There are many parts, yet one body" (1 Co 12:20).

- The Communion of Saints is the definitive expression of the human call to communion.
- It's the unity in "one body" of all who respond to the wedding invitation of the Lamb (see Rev 19).
- We will see all and be seen by all. We will know all and be known by all. And God will be "all in all" (Eph 1:23).

**3a.** *"For man*, this consummation will be the final realization of the unity of the human race, which God willed from creation. ...Those who are united with Christ will form the community of the redeemed, 'the holy city' of God, 'the Bride, the wife of the Lamb'" (CCC, n. 1045).

CYCLE 4: CHRISTIAN CELIBACY

## 4. Eunuchs "for the Kingdom"

Some "have made themselves eunuchs for the sake of the kingdom of heaven" (Mt 19:12).

- A eunuch is someone physically incapable of sexual relations.
- A eunuch "for the kingdom" is someone who freely forgoes sexual relations in order to devote all of his energies and desires to the union that alone can satisfy.
- Those who are celibate for the kingdom "skip" the sacrament in anticipation of the ultimate reality, the "Marriage of the Lamb."
- In this way they boldly proclaim that "the kingdom of God is here."

**4a.** Christ's words "clearly indicate the importance of the personal choice and also the ...particular grace" of this vocation (TB, 263).

**4b.** In the Latin Church, priests "are normally chosen from among men of faith who live a celibate life and who intend to remain celibate 'for the sake of the kingdom of heaven'" (CCC, n. 1579).

## 5. Christian Celibacy Flows from the Redemption of Sexuality

Without understanding the call to redemption, we inevitably look at marriage as a legitimate "outlet" for lust and at celibacy as hopelessly repressive.

- Christ calls *everyone* to experience "liberation from lust" through the redemption of the body.
- Only through this liberation do the Christian vocations (celibacy *and* marriage) make sense.
- Without this liberation, choosing celibacy for one's entire life is absurd. With it, not only does it become possible; it becomes quite attractive.

**5a.** "Adultery in the heart is committed not only because man 'looks' in this way at a woman who is not his wife.... Even if he looked in this way at his wife, he could likewise commit adultery 'in his heart'" (TB, 157).

**5b.** The celibate must submit "the sinfulness of his [fallen] nature to the forces that spring from the mystery of the redemption of the body ...just as any other man does" (TB, 275).

## 6. Christian Celibacy Expresses the Nuptial Meaning of the Body

We can't escape the nuptial meaning of our bodies without doing violence to our humanity.

- Celibacy is *not* a rejection of sexuality, but a living out of the deepest meaning of sexuality – union with Christ and his Church (see Eph 5:31-32).
- Every man is called in some way to be both a husband and a father.
- Every woman is called in some way to be both a wife and a mother.

**6a.** On "the basis of the same nuptial meaning of [the] body ...there can be formed the love that commits man to marriage for the whole duration of his life, but there can be formed also the love that commits man to a life of continence 'for the sake of the kingdom of heaven'" (TB, 284). Celibacy for the kingdom "has acquired the significance of an act of nuptial love" (TB, 282).

**6c.** The celibate person "has the knowledge of being able ...to fulfill himself 'differently' and, in a certain way, 'more' than through matrimony, becoming a 'true gift to others'" (TB, 274).

# Study Questions–Talk #4
# The Heavenly Marriage & the Joy of Christian Celibacy

1. Christopher West posits that when we lose sight of our destiny (i.e. communion with God in heaven), we can make the sexual relationship (which is just the icon or "image" of the heavenly marriage to come) an idol that is worshipped. If this is true, how can this effect marriages, dating relationships, or the discernment of a celibate vocation?

2. What is the Beatific Vision? How was it foreshadowed from the beginning in the union of man and woman?

3. What is a "eunuch for the Kingdom"?

4. What is your initial reaction to Christ's teaching that there will be no marriage in heaven?

5. According to John Paul II, how is celibacy not a rejection of sexuality, but a living out of the deepest meaning of sexuality?

6. What are the supernatural reasons (versus the temporal reasons) for a celibate priesthood?

7. Does the world see marriage as a legitimate outlet for lust? If so, what might be the ramifications of this?

8. How can someone commit "adultery in the heart" with his or her own spouse?

9. How is every man called in some way to be a husband and father? How is every woman called in some way to be a wife and mother?

*Talk 5*

# The Two Become "One Flesh":

*Living the "Great Mystery" of Marriage*

Cycle 5: Christian Marriage

**1. Reverence for Christ**

"Be subject to one another out of reverence for Christ. As the church is subject to Christ, so let wives also be subject in everything to their husbands. Husbands, love your wives, as Christ loved the church and gave himself up for her" (Eph 5: 21, 24-25).

- According to the analogy, the wife is a symbol of the Church and the husband is a symbol of Christ.

- Christ came not to *be* served *but to serve* – to lay down His life for His Bride (see Mt 20:28).

- St. Paul *does not justify male domination.* This is the result of sin (see Gen 3:16).

- St. Paul is seeking to restore the original order *before* sin.

**1a.** Marriage "corresponds to the vocation of Christians only when it reflects the love which Christ the Bridegroom gives to the Church his Bride, and which the Church ...attempts to return to Christ" (TB, 312).

**1b.** Christians "must no longer live as the Gentiles do." They "are darkened in their understanding ...due to their hardness of heart." So put off "your old nature which ...is corrupt through deceitful lusts, ...and put on the new nature, created after the likeness of God in true righteousness and holiness" (Eph 4:17-18, 22-24).

**1c.** Since the "submission of the Church to Christ ...consists in experiencing His love," we can conclude that "the wife's 'submission' to her husband ...signifies above all 'the experiencing of love'" (TB, 320).

**1d.** "So therefore that 'reverence for Christ' ...of which [St. Paul] speaks, is none other than a spiritually mature form of that mutual attraction: man's attraction to femininity and woman's attraction to masculinity" (TB, 379).

**1e.** If a husband is truly to love his wife, "it is necessary to insist that intercourse must not serve merely as a means of allowing [his] climax. ...The man must take [the] difference between male and female reactions into account ...so that climax may be reached [by] both ...and as far as possible occur in both simultaneously." The husband must do this "not for hedonistic, but for altruistic reasons." In this case, if "we take into account the shorter and more violent curve of arousal in the man, [such] tenderness on his part in the context of marital intercourse acquires the significance of an act of virtue" (LR, 272, 275).

## 2. Prototype of All the Sacraments

According to the spousal analogy, the purpose of the sacraments is to unite us with Christ the Bridegroom and "impregnate" us with divine life.

- Marriage, then, is not only one of the seven sacraments, but serves as a kind of model for all the sacraments.
- This is why the Church so diligently safeguards the meaning of marriage.
- When we redefine marriage, with the same stroke we "redefine" Christianity.
- When we redefine marriage, we redefine the very meaning of our humanity.

**2a.** "The entire Christian life bears the mark of the spousal love of Christ and the Church. Already Baptism ...is a nuptial mystery; it is so to speak the nuptial bath which precedes the wedding feast, the Eucharist" (CCC, n. 1617).

**2b.** *"The Eucharist is the... sacrament of the Bridegroom and the Bride"* (MD, n. 26).

**2c.** All "the sacraments of the new covenant find in a certain sense their prototype in marriage" (TB, 339). "The Church cannot therefore be understood ...unless we keep in mind the 'great mystery' ...expressed in the 'one flesh' [union] of marriage and the family" (LF, n. 19).

**2d.** What we learn in Ephesians 5 is obviously "important in regard to marriage." However it "is equally essential ...for the understanding of man in general: for the ...self-comprehension of his being in the world" (TB, 352-353).

## 3. The Language of the Body

"'For this reason a man shall leave his father and mother and be joined to his wife, and the two shall become one flesh.' This is a great mystery, and I mean in reference to Christ and the church" (Eph 5:21-33).

- The body has a "language" that's meant to proclaim the truth of God's love poured out in Christ's body "given up" for us.

**NOTES**

- Christ's love is *free, total, faithful,* and *fruitful*.

- This is precisely what spouses commit to at the altar, and this is precisely what they're meant to express when they become "one flesh."

- Intercourse, therefore, is where the words of the wedding vows *become flesh*.

**3a.** The "very words 'I take you to be my wife – my husband' ...can be fulfilled only by means of conjugal intercourse." Here "we pass to the reality which corresponds to these words" (TB, 355).

**3b.** "As ministers of a sacrament which is constituted by consent and perfected by conjugal union, man and woman are called to express that mysterious 'language' of their bodies in all the truth which is proper to it. By means of gestures and reactions, by means of the whole dynamism ...of tension and enjoyment – whose direct source is the body in its masculinity and its femininity, the body in its action and interaction – by means of all this, ...the person, 'speaks.' ...Precisely on the level of this 'language of the body' ...man and woman reciprocally express themselves in the fullest and most profound way possible to them" (TB, 397-398).

## 4. The Language of the Body is "Prophetic" & "Liturgical"

A prophet is one who proclaims the mystery of God. The liturgy is where we offer our bodies in worship to God.

- But we must be careful to distinguish between true and false prophets (see TB, 365).

- And we must worship God "in spirit and truth" (Jn 4: 23-24).

- If we can speak the truth with our bodies, we can also speak lies.

**4a.** Spouses "are called explicitly to bear witness – by using correctly the 'language of the body' – to spousal and procreative love, a witness worthy of 'true prophets.' In this consists ...the grandeur of [marriage] in the sacrament of the Church" (TB, 365).

**4b.** Through "the 'language of the body' – man and woman encounter the 'great mystery.' ...In this way conjugal life becomes in a certain sense liturgical" (TB, 380).

*See next page for Study Questions*

## Study Questions–Talk #5
## The Two Become "One Flesh":
## Living the "Great Mystery of Marriage

1. How is the wife a symbol of the Church and the husband a symbol of Christ?

2. People tend to react negatively to the verse in Ephesians 5 that speaks of wives being "submissive." How does the Pope explain this spousal "submission" passage in his theology of the body?

3. Why does marriage serve as a model for all the sacraments?

4. Why does the Church teach that only men can be ordained priests?

5. How is Christ's love for us free, total, faithful, and fruitful?

6. What do couples commit to at the altar?

6. How do people speak 'truth' with their bodies as well as 'lies'?

NOTES

*Talk 6*
# Authentic Chastity:

*From Legalism to Liberty*

**1. Chastity & Sexual Freedom**

How often is chastity considered something negative – a long list of oppressive "thou shalt nots"?

- Remember, Christ didn't come to give us more rules to follow (legalism).
- Christ came to transform our hearts so we would no longer need the rules (liberty).
- Mature chastity is not oppressive legalism, but true sexual liberation!

**1a.** "Chastity is very often understood as ...one long 'no.' Whereas it is above all the 'yes' of which certain 'no's' are the consequence" (LR, 170).

Society talks a lot about "sexual freedom." But this typically refers to unrestrained indulgence.

- Is an alcoholic who cannot say "no" to his next drink free?
- Society's concept of sexual freedom actually promotes *addiction* – bondage to lust.
- True freedom is liberation not from the *external* "constraint" that calls me to good, but from the *internal* constraint that hinders my choice of the good.

**1b.** "The virtuous man is he who freely practices the good" (CCC, n. 1804).

**1c.** Those bound by lust "experience God's law as a burden, and indeed as ...a restriction of their own freedom. On the other hand, those who are impelled by love ...feel an interior urge... not to stop at the minimum demands of the Law, but to live them in their 'fullness.' This is a still uncertain and fragile journey as long as we are on earth, but it is one made possible by grace" (VS, n. 18)

**1d.** Grace is that mysterious gift made to the human "heart" which frees men and women to become a sincere gift to each other (see TB, 68).

**2. The "Personalistic Norm"**

The guiding principle of all Catholic moral teaching is the dignity of the human person. John Paul II calls this guiding principle the "personalistic norm."

**2a.** This norm, in its negative form, states that persons must never be treated as objects of use, as merely a means to an end. In its positive form the personalistic norm affirms that love is the only proper attitude towards a person (see LR, p. 41).

## What is love? Is love a feeling? A physical attraction? An emotion?

**2b.** Emotions, feelings, and physical attraction "constitute only the 'raw material' of love. There exists a tendency to regard them as its finished form" (LR, 139). These "components, if they are not [properly] held together ...may add up not to love, but to its direct opposite" (LR, 146).

**2c.** "Sometimes, what is called ... 'love,' if subjected to searching critical examination turns out to be, contrary to all appearances, only a form of 'utilization' of the person" (LR, 167).

**2d.** Lust impels people very powerfully towards physical intimacy. But *if this grows out of nothing more than lust* it is not love. On the contrary it is a negation of love (see LR, 150-151).

**2e.** Authentic love does not say: "I long for you as a good" but "I long for your good," "I long for that which is good for you." The person who truly loves longs for this with no ulterior motive, no selfish consideration. This is the purest form of love and it brings the greatest fulfillment (see LR, 83-84).

## 3. Chastity & the Integration of Love

For love to take root, above all we must firmly set our will on the person's good, utterly refusing to indulge lust. But this does not mean we "stuff" or ignore our emotions and attractions.

- What's needed is integration of emotion and attraction with the dignity of the person.
- This is the role of the virtue of chastity.

**3a.** *"Chastity can only be thought of in association with the virtue of love.* Its function is to free love from the utilitarian attitude." It must control "those centers deep within the human being in which the utilitarian attitude is hatched and grows" (LR, 169, 170).

**3b.** The essence of chastity consists in quickness to affirm the value of the person in every situation, and in raising to the personal level all reactions to a person's body and sex. It is not a matter of "annihilating" sexual reactions or pushing them into the subconscious where they await an opportunity to explode. Chastity is a matter of sustained long term integration of sexual values with the value of the person (see LR, 170-171).

**3c.** "The person [who wants] to succeed in mastering [sexual] impulse and excitement, must be committed to a progressive education in self control of the will, of the feelings, of the emotions; and this education must develop beginning with the most simple acts in which it is relatively easy to put the interior decision into practice" (TB, 408).

## 4. Chaste Love Recognizes the "Unrepeatability" of the Person

Love reaches maturity when it turns from how the other makes me feel to who the other person *is*.

- Every person is totally unique and "unrepeatable."
- No person can ever be compared to another, measured by, or replaced by another.

Authentic love is attracted not just by "attributes" or "qualities" of a person that light a "spark."

- Qualities are *repeatable* – they can always be found in others and to a higher degree.
- If love stops here, a permanent shadow is cast over the permanency of relationship.

**4a.** "Only the value of the person can sustain a stable relationship. The other values of sexuality are wasted away by time and are exposed to the danger of disillusion. But this is not the case for the value of the person, ...which is stable and in some way infinite. When love develops and reaches the person, then it is forever" (KW, 100).

The person who is the object of lust gradually realizes the sentiment of the other:

- "You don't need *me*. You don't desire *me*. You desire only a means of gratification."
- Far from feeling loved and affirmed as a unique and unrepeatable person, those objectified by lust feel used and debased as a repeatable commodity.

**4b.** We often experience sexual stimuli offering equally or more seductive possibilities of new sexual relationships. If the person I "love" is only an instrument for my own pleasure, then he or she can easily be replaced in such a function, a fact which casts a permanent shadow of doubt over the relationship. The case is different when love reaches the person. Then the other is loved not for the quality that he or she has (and which one can lose or which others could have in a higher degree) but for his or her own sake. Only then is their living together something more than the joining of two selfish individuals, and capable of achieving a real personal unity (see KW, 102).

## 5. Ask & You Shall Receive

**5a.** "I thought that [chastity] arose from one's own powers, which I did not recognize in myself. I was foolish enough not to know ...that no one can be [chaste] unless you grant it. For you would surely have granted it if my inner groaning had reached your ears and I with firm faith had cast my cares on you" (St. Augustine, CCC, n. 2520).

Ask and you shall receive. What father among you, if his son asks for a fish will give him a serpent? How much more will the Heavenly Father give the Holy Spirit to those who ask him (see Lk 11:9-13)?

> *Heavenly Father, we ask your forgiveness for ever doubting your love for us, for ever thinking that turning from your plan for our lives, for our sexuality, would somehow bring us happiness. Recognizing our own weaknesses, with bold confidence we ask you for the gift of a chaste heart. Pour out your life and your love on each of us gathered here. Set our desires aright. Teach us to love as you love. Amen.*

## Study Questions–Talk #6
## Authentic Chastity:
## From Legalism to Liberty

1. What is the positive meaning of chastity? Who does this term apply to?

2. What is the difference between society's definition of "sexual freedom" and the freedom spoken of in this talk?

3. Oftentimes what is perceived as 'love' is actually 'lust', especially in today's media. Articulate the traits of each. Discuss how lust can so easily be disguised as love.

4. What is the difference between legitimate passionate love ("eros") and lust?

5. What does it mean when we say that each person is "unrepeatable"?

6. *Memorize* the "personalistic norm", that we may be reminded to always uphold the dignity of each human person!

NOTES

*Created & Redeemed – Page 28*

*Talk 7*

# Theology in the Bedroom:

*Love, Sex, & Fertility*

### Cycle 6: Sexual Morality & Procreation

**1. Sexual Honesty**

"This is my commandment, that you love one another as I have loved you" (Jn 15:12).

- All questions of sexual morality come down to one basic question.
- Is this an authentic sign of God's *free, total, faithful, fruitful* love or is it not?
- In other words, is this a faithful expression of wedding vows or is it not?

> **1a.** We "can speak of moral good and evil" in the sexual relationship "according to whether ...or not it has the character of the truthful sign" (TB, 141-142).

Simply getting married doesn't automatically guarantee sexual honesty. For example, if spouses are just going through the motions and don't *mean* what they're saying – or worse, if they're in some way trying to *cancel* what their union means – then they are being sexually dishonest.

> **1b.** The spouses' effort to make their sexual union a faithful expression of their marriage commitment presents "the internal problem of every marriage" (LR, 225).

**2. The Contradiction of Contraception**

To contradict means to "speak *against*." Contra-ception is a *contra-diction* of the very language of marital love. It turns the "I do" of wedding vows into an "I do *not*."

> **1c.** The language of the body has "clear-cut meanings" all of which are "'programmed' ...in the conjugal consent." For example, to "the question: 'Are you willing to accept responsibly and with love the children that God may give you...?'" – the man and the woman reply: 'Yes'" (TB, 363, 364).

Not only does contraception speak against the commitment to remain open to children. A closer look reveals that it contradicts each of the elements of the marriage commitment.

- *Free:* Contraception was not invented to prevent pregnancy! We already had a 100% safe, 100% reliable way of doing that.
- *Total:* Contracepted intercourse says, "I give myself to you totally... *no I don't.*"
- *Faithful:* How can we speak of fidelity when we're violating freedom, total self-giving, and openness to children?

## 3. Responsible Parenthood

It's a myth that the Church teaches couples are obligated to have as many children as is physically possible. The Church calls couples to a *responsible* exercise of parenthood.

> **3a.** Those "are considered 'to exercise responsible parenthood who prudently and generously decide to have a large family, or who, for serious reasons and with due respect to the moral law, choose to have no more children for the time being or even for an indeterminate period'" (TB, 394).

So, what could a couple do if they had a "serious reason" to avoid a child that wouldn't violate the meaning of intercourse as a sign of God's love?

- Abstaining from intercourse is in no way contraceptive.
- Contraception is the choice to engage in an act of intercourse but *render* it sterile.
- In order to render an act of intercourse sterile (in order to contracept), you must first engage in the act.
- Abstinence is the choice not to "speak" rather than to "speak-*against.*"

Another question arises. Would a couple be doing anything to violate their wedding vows if they had intercourse on a day on which they knew they were naturally infertile?

- Herein lies the principle of Natural Family Planning (NFP).
- NFP is acceptable not because it's "natural" as opposed to "artificial," but because it is in keeping with the nature of sexual intercourse as a renewal of the couple's wedding vows.
- Never does a couple using NFP do anything to sterilize their acts of intercourse. If pregnancy does not result

from their acts of intercourse, it's *God's* doing, not *their* doing. Every time such a couple have intercourse they can honestly pray, "Lord, your will be done."

**3b.** The difference between contraception and periodic abstinence "is much wider and deeper than is usually thought, one which involves in the final analysis two irreconcilable concepts of the human person and of human sexuality" (FC, n. 32).

**3c.** Even "when procreation is not possible, conjugal life does not for this reason lose its value. Physical sterility in fact can be ...the occasion for other important services to the life of the human person, for example, adoption, various forms of educational work, and assistance to other families and to poor or handicapped children" (FC, 14).

## 4. A Question of Faith

Many object that the Church's teaching doesn't correspond to our real possibilities.

- Remember, Christ reveals "another vision of man's possibilities."

- We must be careful not to fall into the trap of "holding the form of religion" while "denying the power of it" (2 Tim 3:5).

- It's a question of faith: do we believe that Christ can empower us to love as he loves or do we not? Is redemption a sham?

**4a.** What "are the 'concrete possibilities of man'? And of which man are we speaking? Of man *dominated* by lust or of man *redeemed by Christ*? This is what is at stake: the *reality* of Christ's redemption. *Christ has redeemed us!* This means He has given us the possibility of realizing the *entire truth* of our being; He has set our freedom free from the *domination* of [lust]. And if redeemed man still sins, this is not due to an imperfection of Christ's redemptive act, but to man's will not to avail himself of the grace which flows from that act. God's command is of course proportioned to man's capabilities; but to the capabilities of the man to whom the Holy Spirit has been given" (VS, n. 103).

*See next page for Study Questions*

# Study Questions–Talk #7
# Theology in the Bedroom:
# Love, Sex & Fertility

1. What do you understand the Church to teach in the area of marital love and openness to children?

    - Does the Church expect married couples to have as many children as possible?
    - Are children the only expression of "fruitfulness" in marriage?

2. What is the one question that helps determine the morality of a sexual act?

3. How do we apply the criteria of free, total, faithful, and fruitful love to the following:

    - contraception
    - in vitro fertilization
    - homosexual acts
    - pornography
    - masturbation

4. Most people look at contraception as simply a means of avoiding pregnancy. What are some of the unintended consequences of contraception on marriage and society?

5. How does abstaining from fertile intercourse (i.e. Natural Family Planning) differ from using contraceptives?

6. Many insist that the Church should "get out of my bedroom" and "get with the times". What is at the root of these sentiments and how does the theology of the body help us to address those who feel this way?

7. Christ came not to condemn, but to save (see Jn. 3:17). How, then, is the Church's teaching on sexual morality a message of salvation?

## Talk 8

# "Put out into the Deep":

*The New Evangelization*

### 1. The Driving Force of Culture

During the Bush-Gore "chad saga" in 2000, Francis Fukuyama, professor of public policy at George Mason University, wrote an article for the *Wall Street Journal* entitled "What Divides America."

- The real debate, he argued, is not over foreign policy or the economy.
- The real issues, he believes, are social and cultural ones.

**1a.** "The single most important social change to have taken place in the United States over the past forty years concerns sex and the social role of women, and it is from this single source that virtually all of the 'culture wars' stem. Uncomfortable as it may be to acknowledge this fact, the breakdown of the nuclear family, reflected in rising divorce rates, illegitimacy and cohabitation in place of marriage, stems from two sources: the movement of women into the paid labor force, and the separation of sex from reproduction thanks to birth control and abortion" (*Wall Street Journal*; Nov 15, 2000, p. A26).

Here we find confirmation from a secular source of one of John Paul II's deepest convictions: "The driving force which shapes history is not politics or economics or military might. It is culture" (SL, 346). And the driving force of culture, as always, is sex, marriage, and the family.

- There will be no renewal of the Church and of the world without a renewal of marriage and the family.
- There will be no renewal of marriage and the family without a return to the full truth of God's plan for the body and sexuality.
- But this won't happen without a fresh proposal that compellingly demonstrates to the modern world how the Christian sexual ethic – far from the cramped, prudish list of prohibitions it's assumed to be – is a liberating message of *salvation* that corresponds perfectly with the desires of the human heart.
- This is the great gift of John Paul II's "theology of the body."

**1b.** "If we look at today's world, we are struck by many negative factors that can lead to pessimism. But this feeling is unjustified: we have faith in God our Father and Lord and in his mercy. ...God is preparing a great springtime for Christianity, and we can already see its first signs" (RM, n. 86)

**1c.** The theology of the body is "one of the boldest reconfigurations of Catholic theology in centuries" – "a kind of *theological time bomb* set to go off with dramatic consequences ...perhaps in the twenty-first century" (WH, 336, 343).

## 2. What is the New Evangelization?

What is "new" about this evangelization is not the message.

- "Jesus Christ is the same yesterday, today, and forever" (Heb 13:8).
- What's "new" is that it is directed not only toward the unbaptized, but towards the modern phenomenon of the "baptized non-believer."

**3a.** What is essential in order to meet the unprecedented needs of our day is a proclamation of the Gospel that is "new in ardor, methods, and expression" (John Paul II address March 9, 1983)

**3b.** The *"new evangelization* [involves] a vital effort to come to a deeper understanding of the mysteries of faith and to find meaningful language with which to convince our contemporaries that they are called to newness of life through God's love." It is the task of sharing with modern men and women "the 'unsearchable riches of Christ' and of making known 'the plan of the mystery hidden for ages in God who created all things' (Eph 3:8-9)" (SE, pp. 53, 55).

## 4. The Theology of the Body "Incarnates" the Gospel

John Paul's theology of the body demonstrates that the Gospel is not "out there" somewhere. God's mystery is stamped right in us – in our deepest spiritual longings for intimacy and communion and in our very bodies as male and female.

- The new evangelization is not first an appeal to abstract principles, but to the desires of the human heart for love and communion – and the compelling witness that Jesus is the answer to that longing for communion.
- Christ fully reveals man to himself and makes his supreme calling (communion) clear!

**4a.** "God comes to us in the things we know best and can verify most easily, the things of our everyday life, apart from which we cannot understand ourselves" (FR, n. 12).

**4b.** "To make the Church *the home and school of communion*: that is the great challenge facing us in the millennium which is now beginning, if we wish to be faithful to God's plan and respond to the world's deepest yearnings" (NMI, n. 43).

**4c.** "We need to bring the *Gospel of life* to the heart of every man and woman and to make it penetrate every part of society. This involves above all proclaiming *the core* of this Gospel. It is the proclamation of a living God who is close to us, who calls us to profound communion with himself and awakens in us the certain hope of eternal life. It is the affirmation of the inseparable connection between the person, his life and his bodiliness. It is the presentation of human life as a life of relationship, a gift of God, the fruit and sign of his love. It is the proclamation that Jesus has a unique relationship with every person, which enables us to see in every human face the face of Christ. It is the call for a 'sincere gift of self' as the fullest way to realize our personal freedom. [As a consequence] the meaning of life is found in giving and receiving love, and in this light human sexuality and procreation reach their true and full significance" (EV, n. 81).

## 5. Put Out into the Deep

In the story of the miraculous catch of fish, when Christ asked the disciples to lower their nets, it was Peter who responded with faith, "At your word I will let down the nets" (Lk 5:5).

Two thousand years later, the successor of Peter is calling us to respond with faith.

- Yet if there is to be a great catch of fish in a "new evangelization," Christians must first recover the sense of having an urgently important message for the salvation of the world.
- The "Gospel of the body" proclaimed by John Paul II is that message. *How urgently it is needed!*

I appeal to you – take up this theology of the body. Make it your mission in life to know it, live it, and share it with everyone you know. If we do that, the "new springtime" will come to full flowering.

**5a.** "We are certainly not seduced by the naive expectation that, faced with the great challenges of our time, we shall find some magic formula. No, we shall not be saved by a formula, but by a Person, and the assurance which he gives us: *I am with you!*" (NMI, n. 29). Christ the Bridegroom is with us! (see LF, part II)

This is our living hope! If we share this hope with the world, we shall not fall short of renewing the face of the earth. Amen.

*See next page for Study Questions*

# Study Questions–Talk #8
# "Put out into the Deep":
# The New Evangelization

1. What role do you think John Paul II's Theology of the Body has in building a culture of life?

2. In light of what you have learned throughout this study, do you believe that George Weigel's statements below are true or not? Explain your reasoning.

   - "John Paul's portrait of sexual love as an icon of the interior life of God has barely begun to shape the Church's theology, preaching, and religious education. When it does, it will compel a dramatic development of thinking about virtually every major theme in the Creed."

   - The Theology of the Body is "one of the boldest reconfigurations of Catholic theology in centuries."

   - The Theology of the Body is "a kind of theological time bomb set to go off with dramatic consequences ... perhaps in the twenty-first century" (WH, 343).

3. How has participating in this study affected you? What do you plan to do from here?

4. In light of your understanding of the theology of the body, consider again the following questions:

   - Where do I come from and why do I exist?
   - What is the meaning of life and how do I live it?
   - What is my ultimate destiny and how do I attain it?
   - Why is there evil in the world and how do I overcome it?

---

### Acknowledgements
*Created & Redeemed Study Guide* written by Christopher West. *Created & Redeemed Study Guide* questions written by Christopher West, Matthew Pinto and Jennifer Messing.

# NOTES